The Problem Deaf Child

This book is dedicated to
George R. Martens
Father of George and Irene

The Problem Deaf Child

A New Approach and the Color System

By
Ernest Tinsmith
and
Katherine J. Martens

 FUTURA
PUBLISHING COMPANY
1974

Contents

Foreword

Education of the deaf child is a long and tedious task that is often frustrating to the educator and the child, with slow progress toward long range goals.

The Tinsmith—Martens color system offers parents, therapists, and teachers a consistent training program for deaf children that will offer speedy success; thereby motivating trainer and child to continue learning in order to reap greater rewards. Such stimulation and interest in learning when offered at an early age can avoid many of the emotional overlays that accompany poor comprehension and poor self-image. In addition, having a lifeline of communication overcomes many of the confused concepts generally attributed to deaf children.

Within these pages are specific lessons people can follow to establish good language patterns as a guide for the deaf child.

Laura Nadoolman
Principal Hebrew Institute For The Deaf;

Former Supervisor Teacher Training In Deaf Education At New York University.

Introduction

The type of deafness in schools for the deaf has changed in the last fifty years. Due to important discoveries in preventive medicine and medical science, the number of inner ear deaf children is decreasing, and the number of children with cortical speech and hearing problems is increasing.

Beginning in 1953, Professor Ernest Tinsmith* delivered a series of lectures and demonstrations about central speech hearing impairment. He spoke to educators of the deaf and to speech therapists concerning the growing problems in deaf education. At that time, he met with very little understanding and tremendous opposition. Today, however, most of the educators in this field realize that the many difficulties he mentioned exist. Yet, little has been done so far to educate these children. More importantly, how can we best help them in the future?

Children with central hearing impairment are given various labels: "mentally slow," "learning problems," "emotional problems," etc. All of these, in most cases, are merely symptoms of the central hearing impairment. It is the professed

*see Biographical Sketches

opinion of some that many children with this type of impairment have no "speech feeling" and, therefore, cannot be successful with oral language. These children, as a result, are placed in non-oral classes. After many years of experience with such children, Professor Tinsmith states that if one uses the proper teaching method and a good auditory training system, definite success can be achieved. From the standpoint of language, speech, and mental development, many of these children are able to progress to a high level of achievement, and a significant percentage can even advance to standards of excellence.

For the past three years, as Professor Tinsmith's assistant, I have had the opportunity to implement this method and have seen the excellent results it has achieved. In the hope of helping a greater number of children, this book has been prepared. We hope that it will be but the beginning of a more concerted effort to meet this problem.

Katherine J. Martens*

*see Biographical Sketches

Acknowledgments

We wish to thank: Victoria Wagner, former Director of the Ethical Culture Schools for reading and corrections of the final manuscript. Professor Joseph L. Papaleo, Chairman of the Writing Department of Sarah Lawrence College and his wife, Lois for their friendship in addition to valuable assistance in the various stages of the manuscript. Nancy Durso who helped with her typing, her encouragement and her friendship. Marguerite Fields, our colleague, for her support each time it was asked. Our special thanks to: Malcolm Goodman, teacher of Ethics and English at the Fieldston School for his assistance in editing the manuscript.

Problems and Goals

Education is a process through which we develop the mental potentials and qualities in the individual. Through education, man is prepared to find his place in the community.

Our aim is to develop the hearing-impaired child's potential to a level at which he can find his place in the hearing community as a useful citizen, so that he is able to earn his own living and enjoy his environment as well as his hearing peers.

Children, whose lives could not be saved two or three decades ago, are being saved today. Many of these children, owing to serious illnesses, are handicapped or multiple handicapped. They require special assistance through a special approach and method. If we do not admit such children to our schools or dismiss them without giving them every opportunity to develop their innate potential, we are not only failing as educators, but we are facing the prospect of creating a lasting and increasing problem for our educational system and the community, a problem so acute that it deserves more attention than it is receiving at the present time.

Our work with problem children requires love and understanding. An alarming number of these children cannot be taught successfully in regular classes for the deaf. Even after many years of instruction they fail to show progress and have no interest in school work.

One of our desires is to provide the child with a new start and to create for him a congenial atmosphere in the classroom. We must assign him work that he is able to perform and praise him for his effort and achievements.

In order to succeed, the child has to grow fond of his teacher and develop trust in him. When the child has been reached he will want to improve, not for his own sake, but to please his teacher. With time, he will recognize the advantages of learning, and realize that he has a far better chance to reach his goals through the use of speech. He has to learn how to work in a group as a member of a small community and must comply with its demands.

It is our responsibility to develop the potential of the whole human being. We must not only teach subject matter but also help these children to become responsible, independent citizens. To compete successfully in the hearing world, these children must be well prepared.

Our goal, therefore, is a long-range preparation which has to commence on the very first day of school. We cannot afford to waste those important initial years of the child's educational, social, and emotional development.

Due to important discoveries in preventive medicine and medical science, the number of inner ear deaf children is decreasing, while the number of children with cortical speech and hearing problems is increasing.

Most of the children with cortical deafness have emotional problems or seem to be mentally retarded. Many of them cannot profit from the method of instruction which is provided today for inner ear deaf children. When instructed with a method more suitable for them, not only does the child's hearing and speech ability develop, but his mental potential is released and his emotional problems begin to disappear. The child emerges from his passivity and becomes a good student, although he was already marked as a slow learner and a hindrance in the classroom.

Only some of the children with cortical speech and hearing problems can profit from instruction using the lipreading-kinesthetic method alone and are able to learn with inner ear deaf children. Even they, however, are not able to develop their speech-hearing and mental potentials to capacity. Others have serious learning difficulties and do not want to participate in any school work. They consequently appear "slow" or "mentally retarded" and are branded as such. But they can be reached with the proper method of teaching and can be given a chance to lead a purposeful existence. The "four-word system" is the proper approach for beginning our work.

The current definition of a deaf child is, "a normal child who lacks hearing and whose mental development has been handicapped only by this hearing defect." The present-day lip-reading kinesthetic method is supposed to remove the barrier which hinders the normal development of the deaf child's capacities. The current oral method shows fair results with children whose deafness is due to impaired hearing organs.

The fact that only a certain continually decreasing number of children were benefited by this method prompted Dr. Gustav Barczi* to search for the cause of the failure.

The origins of Barczi's research reach back to 1802. In his study of deaf-mutism, Barczi arrived at the conclusion that in the last one hundred years, the disease picture has changed. It is interesting to note the causes of deafness of eighty to one hundred years ago. In that time span, schools for the deaf recorded incidences of infectious disease which caused deafness as a result of total or partial damage to the hearing organs. Deafness could be confirmed otologically in 85% of the cases. The other 15% were of unknown origin. In recent years pre-natal virus infections, such as maternal rubella, have been recognized as important causative factors.

In the case of "Cortical Deafness," the child's auditory capacity is deficient because there is a disturbance in "speech reception," "speech concentration," and "speech memory."

In explaining the condition of deafness in the cortex, we

*See Biographical Sketches

4

egin with a discussion of "aphasia," a comparable disease. Ve now know that the functions of hearing and speech comrise a much larger part of the cortex than was thought some me ago. If a physiological disturbance occurs in one part of 1e frontal lobes, a speech or hearing defect appears. In dults "aphasia" can be produced by such disturbances as ıptured blood vessels or serious head injuries. Autopsies on ersons who were afflicted with "aphasia" disclose that lood vessels in one part of the frontal lobes are filled with lood, bloodclots, or air.

In the case of "Deafness in the Cortex," the child has no :onception of voice or any idea of what speech is. Therefore, f sound (speech) reaches the cortex, the brain can do nothng with these impressions because it does not have the necesary readiness, or energy, to receive them and to preserve hem in memory. In such a case, the brain cell has a lower ralue of so-called "energetical readiness." With "stimulaion," however, it moves to its "physiological limit"; the ɔrain's "compensating power" can come into action as it loes in the "Agraphia," "Alexia," and "Acalculia" cases vherein correction is possible.

Hearing is a process which is closely connected with learnng. In the cases of "Deafness of the Cortex," we are confronted with a brain which is capable of receiving sound and speech, but one which is unable to integrate them because :he impression is either too complicated or too weak to be noticed and retained. It is necessary, therefore, to evolve a system by which the auditory center can be stimulated to receive sound and to note the differences between sounds and sound groups which, basically, is speech.

Such a system is based upon oral, rhythmic exercises, the physiology of sound, and the "global method," which is based on the audio-visual tactile sense.

The sense of touch, certainly, is more primitive than the sense of hearing. Some sound waves do in fact reach our brain center through "bone-conduction." This is the "Schwabach reaction."

Awakening of Hearing

We begin our work of "awakening the hearing" only after an otological examination has indicated that there is no inflammation of the ear. This is because the method depends on speaking directly into the child's ear.

The first words we use, which lead to the excitement of the "tactile sense" (sense of touch), make discrimination possible.

The four words which we place before the child must have good (1) staccato rhythm; (2) dynamic power; (3) different vowels; (4) kinesthetic feeling; (5) visualization when written or read.

We start with words which are easily pronounced and heard, such as: bow, home, bus, two, butter, baby, puppy, arm, yellow, bee, down, out, tomorrow, apple, tomato, hello, come, go, get, window, you, Saturday, Sunday, me, book, open, today, four, shoe—the actual choice depending upon the teacher.

We place the four words before the child and give the words through lipreading. (We do not waste much time at this stage.) We give the meaning through pictures or dramatization and use flashcards with pictures or words.

| bee | home |
| baby | apple |

We say the words one by one directly into the child's ear in order to lead to the excitement of the tactile sense. (Later the method we employ is to place a sheet of paper between our face and the child's ear in such a way as to obstruct the child's vision and tactile sense.) We say a word into his ear and ask for the corresponding printed word or picture. When the child can point to the words, we put four new words before him and repeat this procedure in the same manner until he has forty to fifty words. We do not overload him but proceed slowly and say one word many times into the child's ear.

When the child can hear forty to fifty words and can say and use them in his daily life, he is ready to start building sentences.

Each word has a lipreading kinesthetic value, a sound value, and a meaning.

We give as much sound value as possible to the child's speech. A deaf child's speech has as much value as the intelligibility of his speech to a hearing person.

In auditory training, it makes no difference if the child is cortically deaf or has residual hearing. We have to work with both in the same way. The cortically deaf will generally develop better hearing and will have a more pleasant voice quality. The hard-of-hearing child will develop better speech only in the healthy parts of the cochlea where hearing control is possible.

At this stage of hearing awakening we teach forty to fifty words by using the four word system. This kind of stimulation of the speech-hearing center needs long and hard work until the brain is willing to receive the word (sound group) and retain it in memory. The tape recorder can be of use in this work to provide the repetitive stimulation of the cortex.

Speech and Auditory Training

If the child is able to hear and repeat words which have different vowels, such as u, ä, ō, ü, the child is in the "primary auditory stage." The hearing of ā, ē, a, e vowels puts the child into the second stage. Hearing of the vowels already is effective hearing. The hearing of consonants is "combinable hearing." The development of "combinable hearing" and "speech ability" are the ways to achieve oral communication.

If a child does not have pleasant voice quality, we have to help him to attain normal pitch. The child will use normal pitch when crying or laughing. We must work toward maintaining this pitch in all speech work. Rhythm and emphasis can be worked on later.

At the time of puberty, the child's pitch changes. It is important to control and, if needed, to correct pitch at this stage.

Some of our children have a high and unpleasant voice quality. Such a child can hear himself at this pitch, but only at this pitch, because it is the healthy part in his cochlea through which he controls his speech. In most of these cases, it is almost impossible to bring the child's voice to the normal level because he likes to hear and control himself, and will insist on using the pitch where he can do so.

As was mentioned earlier, hearing is acquired to a large degree through learning. A young deaf child has only a few or no hearing impressions. At the first stage of auditory training, we have to put words into the speech-hearing center with the "four-word system." We have to develop the child's speech memory. He will hear only those words which he had learned and already has in his speech-hearing center. Therefore, if a hearing aid or head phones are placed on the child prematurely, he will receive only disturbing sounds. We must develop the combinable hearing ability to enable him to hear not only the words which he had learned before, but many more words independently.

We give the child confidence and encourage him to express himself orally. We teach the vowel and consonant charts and expect good pronunciation. To help him see and say the isolated sounds in words, we show him how to find different consonants or vowels and teach the isolated sounds not by their name in the alphabet (e.g., be) but by their phonetic sounds (e.g., bu-bu-bu).

We write three words using:

b	d	h	s	sh
bow	said	home	bus	shoe
tub	do	ham	sweet	washer
baby	daddy	his	Susan	fish

We teach the vowel chart in the same way, using vowel symbols and words.

The Color ABC's

For better results, in speech and hearing, we developed a color speech system. We are using three colors: red for voice, blue for breath, and brown for nasal sounds. The three colors have been used in American and European schools for speech training for many decades. We developed the color alphabet for better pronunciation, applying the Thorndike-Barnhart system:

```
a b c d e f g hij k l m n
o pq r s tu v w x y z
```

The child with speech and hearing problems has to be able to differentiate between the red, the blue, and the brown letters. If he writes "come" (four letters), he has to know that he is writing four. But the word "come" contains only three sounds: "kum"—a blue k, a red u, and a brown m. If he spells bought, he is writing six letters, but will pronounce only three sounds: "bôt"—a red b, a red o, and a blue t.

The color system is important from the standpoints of speech, hearing, and reading. How can we expect a deaf or cortically deaf child to say three or four sounds if we are writing six or seven letters? The color speech system aids the child to achieve better speech.

10

Speech and Language Work

Speech and language are not knowledge, but art and ability. We teach speech and language through developing abilities, through doing, through experience, through imitation, e.g., piano playing, carpentry.

A deaf child cannot develop speech and language the natural way (through hearing speech and language patterns). A deaf child has to learn language art with the help of drill work. This drill work has to carry over into life situations. The problem children need an even simpler approach, the "four-word system."

We teach words and sentences from the child's daily life and use words that he needs.

We encourage the child to speak or write about his feelings, thoughts, and wishes in good language forms.

Each new language form has to be taught systematically with the global method. This means the audio-visual-tactile way, combined with dramatization and sentence building, both in oral and in written form.

Using the Color System, we teach the child to:
1) hear words;
2) hear and build sentences from the learned words;
3) build sentences using different language forms (by, in, at, etc.);
4) hear phrases and complete these in a sentence. For example: We say, "For the baby." He can say, "I bought a doll for the baby," with intelligible speech.

We also:
    give questions and expect proper answers;
    give commands the child has to carry out. For example, "Put the pencil on the table."

We teach the child to express the same thought in different ways. We create pleasant situations in our classroom. Our work has to be lively, interesting, and full of action.

Lipreading

Lipreading is important even for a cortically deaf child, for, as was mentioned previously, the hearing stimulation moves to a physiological limit.

Some cortically deaf children have no "lipreading feeling," but with the development of the hearing through the stimulation system, the child does begin to lipread. Sometimes, not only does the speech-hearing center have damage or a functional loss, but the visual area is also defective. The child cannot see combinations of movements. This is recognized by the child's inability to copy simple shapes and imitate simple combinations of finger movements (for example: to touch repeatedly the left palm held vertically with the right index finger pointing horizontally). Such children also have writing difficulties. To develop the visual center, we have to use simple drawings, writing of capital letters, and combined body movements. This inability is rapidly correctable.

Sign language and speech are expressive movements through which we communicate our thoughts, feelings, and desires. Sign language is concrete, while oral language, a vocalized signing which uses small movements, is more abstract, more comprehensive, more expressive, and more exact in its construction. Speech is one of the most outstanding human abilities, without which man would never have reached today's advanced culture.

If speech is vocalized signing, one has to be able to read it off of the lips. Reading is one way to achieve visual understanding, and speech-reading is another.

We have to develop the inborn feelings and ability for speech-reading. The person who reads speech must know the formation of the isolated sound, but more importantly, he has to acquire a faculty for the combinations and assimilations of sound groups in words and sentences. A person who has better imagination and combinable ability is a better lip-reader.

While some children have a greater faculty for lipreading due to inborn imaginative and combinable abilities, others can be taught to develop this by means of visual understanding. A good way of helping poor lipreaders is the "four-word system." A child's ability to lipread develops as his hearing increases.

Reading

Reading is a way of visual understanding and communication. Fingerspelling, lipreading, and sign language are other ways of visual communication. Reading plays a very important part in the life of deaf people. Therefore, teaching of reading is of primary importance in schools for the deaf. Deaf children have to remember visual symbols: letters, finger movements, movements of speech organs, etc.

The average hearing child is able to learn to read and write around the age of six. Before this age, very few children can remember the many symbols used to express thoughts or feelings in written form.

It is very important to develop the habit of reading in deaf children. Most of them are poor readers because they do not have enough words and language forms. A "First Reading Book" written expressly for deaf children would be of the greatest value. The stories contained in it should be interesting, as well as light, and elementary in vocabulary and language forms. If the child discovers that reading is an entertaining experience which offers him pleasure, he will strive for a higher level of reading competence.

Our Approach

We begin by giving the child words that are easy to say hear, read, and write. We put these words on charts and go over them each day. The child must be able to see the word and give its meaning.

A Sample Word Chart

up	bow	baby	mother	come	down
arm	four	bus	Monday	go	yes
apple	one	bee	today	home	half
butter	puppy	yellow	have	two	no
you	out	tomato	like	man	out
hello	ham	window	buy	today	open

We have the children write each of these words in their notebooks five or six times, at the rate of one chart a day. Later, we cover six words and have the children write them from memory, employing the global method (see p. 11). Once the child has a small vocabulary, we build sentences using the words the child has already learned; e.g., "I have a hat"; "I will buy tomatoes"; "The bee is yellow." A hearing child must hear a word many times before his brain can form an engramme of it. Therefore, in order for a hearing impaired child to remember a word, it is even more important for him to see it repeatedly. It is also necessary to have the child repeatedly write the word in order to facilitate memorization.

We have previously mentioned the color speech and language systems which are useful not only with cortically deaf children but also with the inner ear deaf, the mentally slow hearing, and hearing children with learning difficulties. They may also be employed to teach foreign languages. We introduced the color alphabet in the teaching of speech as a way to hear and pronounce words.

Sample lessons for teaching the color "ABC's"

Color the "a b c's"

a b c d e f g
h i j k l m n
o p q r s t u
v w x y z.

Write the alphabet three times.

1. a   b   ___   ___   ___   ___   ___
   h   ___   ___   ___   ___   ___   ___
   o   ___   ___   ___   ___   ___   ___
   v   ___   ___   ___   ___

2. a   b   ___   ___   ___   ___   ___
   ___   i   ___   ___   ___   ___   ___
   ___   p   ___   ___   ___   ___   ___
   ___   w   ___   ___   ___

3. a   ___   ___   ___   ___   ___   ___
   h   ___   ___   ___   ___   ___   ___
   o   ___   ___   ___   ___   ___   ___
   v   ___   ___   ___   ___

Color the letters:

a b d e g i j l m n
c f h k p s t
p b t d, ng, f v s z

17

The Color
Speech System

If we write "one," the child has to point to the red "w," the red "u," and the brown "n" (w u n) on the color alphabet.

If we write the word "laugh" on the blackboard, the child has to find it on the color alphabet chart. He must point to the red "l," red "a," and the blue "f" (l a f). He has to familiarize himself with the color alphabet chart in the same way that a typist familiarizes himself with the keyboard of the typewriter. He must be able to put the word together phonetically and point to each letter easily. The child must become aware of the fact that he may be writing a word with five letters but only hearing three sounds, which may not correspond with the letters that he is writing (e.g., laugh-laf, one-wun, bought-bôt, come-kum).

The child must know that he says a word the way that he hears it, but not necessarily the way that he sees it. Therefore, all the words must be given in this manner. We don't teach the diphthongs to beginners in the regular way. We use the color speech system writing the two sounds which are pronounced. For example:

1. Not ī but ặi (ice) not īs but ặis
2. Not ō but ồü (bow) not bō but bồü
3. Not ou but uü (cow) not kou but kuü

After a time, some children with less severe problems can use the diphthongs in the regular way.

We put many samples of the color speech system before the child. We spell the word on one side and put the color word on the other.

A Sample Color Speech Chart:

have (hav)	up (up)
one (wun)	come (kum)
today (tü·dā)	bought (bôt)

The child has to have the color speech charts and the Thorndike-Barnhardt Vowel System with the vowels written in red before him constantly. To simplify the work for the children, we do not use the short a (char). When short a is used, we write the "a" that one finds in flag (flag) can (kan) etc.

The following are some charts using examples of color speech writing. If possible, we use words on the charts to introduce all of the vowels.

ē	bee	(bē)	see	(sē)
ā	say	(sā)	may	(mā)
ä	arm	(ärm)	heart	(härt)
u.	up	(up)	sun	(sun)
ü	two	(tü)	shoe	(shü)
ō	home	(hōm)	go	(gō)

e	nest	(nest)	get	(get)
a	can	(kan)	man	(man)
u	book	(búk)	cook	(kúk)
i	sit	(sit)	miss	(mis)
ė	nurse	(nėrs)	hurt	(hėrt)
ô	ball	(bôl)	dog	(dôg)

The child must be able to write, see, hear, and say the different isolated consonants when they are incorporated within words. This is also a good way for the child to build his vocabulary. We do this in the following way:

We Write Words With:

l	d	m	p	t
1. apple	door	mother	puppy	tree
2. low	body	man	apple	butter
3.				

We teach the vowel chart in the same way, using words containing vowel symbols.

ō	u	ä	ü	a
1. home (hōm)	up (up)	arm (ärm)	two (tü)	can (kan)
2. go (gō)	sun (sun)	palm (päm)	shoe (shü)	man (man)
3.				

In our long experience we have tried many systems for teaching speech and auditory training and have found that we have achieved the best results with our color system.

Auditory Training Lessons

Some lessons for auditory training with the four word system:

	I		
home (hōm)		bee	(bē)
baby (bā-bi)		up	(up)

	II		
bow (bō)		butter	(but-ėr)
puppy (pu-pi)		tomato	(tō-mā-tō)

	III		
tea (tē)		yellow	(ēe-lō)
two (tū)		one	(wun)

	IV		
come (kum)		Monday	(Mun-dā)
go (gō)		blue	(blū)

If the child can hear and say the words which we have already placed into the speech-hearing center, then we can begin to make phrases by connecting two or three words (for example, come up; yellow apple; puppy, come up).

Teaching Colors

We teach colors using the more common ones first

red	purple
blue	white
black	yellow
green	

We then color the balls and balloons.

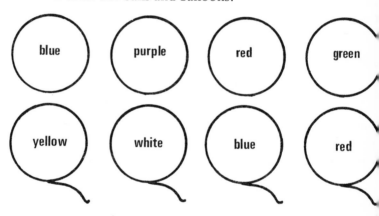

Children enjoy working with colors. Therefore, they find it easy to communicate something about color. For example,

The apple is red.

The ball is yellow.

The tree is green.

In this manner, one can teach the colors and give the child a feeling for building sentences. We write the first sentence on the blackboard: "The apple is red," and draw an apple before the sentence. Then beneath this sentence we draw

22

our lines and place a ball before them.

The apple is red.

___ ___ __ ___ .

The child is then expected to fill in the blanks with the words "The ball is blue.", or whatever color he chooses. We give six or seven sentences in this way with different objects and as many lines next to them as the sentence requires, using longer lines for longer words and shorter lines for shorter words. After a time, when the child has familiarized himself with the colors of the parts of speech, the lines can be made in colors. For example: ___ ___ __ ___

Nouns are red, verbs blue, and adjectives green.

For teaching the plural, the child must know that "a" or "an" means one. If we speak of more than one, the child must know that the noun takes an "s." We also teach a few nouns that have special plural forms such as man-men, child-children, tooth-teeth etc.

Sample Lesson:

I see a ball.

I see three balls.

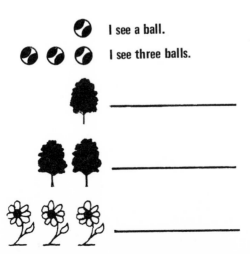

We give numbers to ten.

1 = one	= wun	= •	
2 = two	= tü		= ••
3 = three	= thrē	= •••	

HOW MANY?

0000	= **4**
00000 0	=
000	=
00000 00	=
/////	=
///// /////	=
///// //	=
	=
	=

The Color Language System

Red - Nouns **and** Pronouns
Blue - Verbs
Green - Adjectives
Brown - Prepositions

We build the child's sentence structure through his feelings and desires so that he will be able to think in oral language. Language structure is complicated for a hearing-impaired child, because he cannot absorb it as does a hearing person. The color language system structures language through visualization, thereby making it easier for the child to understand and to remember.

The child has to see such every-day words as: go, play, good, bad, ham, butter, milk, etc. on permanent charts. To organize language in the child's mind, these words must be categorized and written in color. The categories would be food, clothing, body, etc. (which are nouns and written in red), verbs (blue), adjectives (green), and prepositions (brown). As previously mentioned, a child who cannot receive language adequately through his hearing must compensate visually. To do this, he must have the same word groups before him for many months. When visualization is made clearer through colors, the child acquires expressive language. For systematic language work, we begin by giving the child four words, two verbs and two prepositions in color. We begin with the words which we have already used in auditory training.

come   up

go   out

25

The child has to build phrases from these four words and these phrases should also be given through auditory training.

1. come up
2. go out
3. come out
4. get up

Next we put three nouns, three verbs, and three prepositions before the child.

Mary	come	in
puppy	go	up
baby	will	out

1. Puppy go out.
2. Mary will go out.
3. Baby go up.
4._____
5._____

In this way we give the child more words and have him build sentences.

The children have time to do many things during the long school day. We begin our language work with the "News," which consists of six or seven sentences. We do not begin writing the "News" until the first month of school has passed and the children have acquired some vocabulary. They can write such things as:

1. **Today is Monday.**

2. **It is cold.**

3. **It is 8:30.**

4. **Bruce is sick.**

5. **He is at home.**

6. **Bobby has new brown shoes.**

We keep the sentences simple and add any new words to a chart. From these new words we will eventually develop the permanent color charts that were mentioned previously. The new words should be seen, heard, written, and said many times. A child enjoys communicating stories about his home-life and school events and even likes relating things about his dreams. We encourage him to express himself, and help him to use the vocabulary that he has already acquired. Encouragement and help from the teacher are very necessary at this time so that the child will gain the confidence and desire to express himself. There are personality differences amongst children. Because some are outgoing, they will have much to say. We encourage the quiet child to tell his stories too.

Sometimes something exciting will happen to the class. These events make natural topics for discussion, since the interest of the students has already been aroused. We encourage each member of the class to participate to the best of his ability in such discussions.

The Important Verbs

We must give the child awareness of language structure. We do this through the analogy and color systems. We begin with the most useful verbs: "have," "like," "can," "eat," etc. At the same time, we give the personal pronouns: "I," "you," "he," "she," "it," and "we." The plural "you" and "they" are given later. We connect the verb "have" with clothing:

Have	Has
1. I have a tie.	1. Mary has a new ball.
2. I have a dress.	2. Father has a new car.
3. I have	3. _____
4. I _____	4. _____
5. _____	5. _____

28

We connect the verb "can" with verbs connoting abilities such as "jump," "swim," "run," etc.

Can

1. I can run.
2. Larry can play ball.
3. My mother can cook.

4. My teacher can drive.
5. _____
6. _____

We teach the personal pronouns with "have" and "has":

I have _____
He has _____
It has _____

You have _____
She has _____
We have _____

Write sentences with:

I have

1. _____
2. _____
3. _____

She has

1. _____
2. _____
3. _____

I can

1. _____
2. _____
3. _____

Father can

1. _____
2. _____
3. _____

We give the following type of exercise to the children to re-enforce the gender of pronouns:

After a time we put up the first permanent color Verb Chart which consists of the following verbs:

		Verbs	
		drink	love
go	get	see	run
come	write	have	jump
play	read	like	make
work	sleep	can	dream
wash	do	sew	fall
eat	walk	cry	know
fly	talk	laugh	take
buy	give	will	hear

This chart consists of words which the child needs. Some words will be familiar and some will be new to him. The teacher can write sentences using these new verbs.

1. Give me a pen.
2. Don't cry.
3. Get up.
4. Father will go to work.
5. Mother can sew.

Important Topics (Nouns)

At this stage, we also teach the parts of the body. We put the permanent body chart before the children, as well as a picture of a body with each part labeled.

Body			
		elbow	palm
ear	tooth	hand	leg
nose	teeth	thumb	knee
hair	neck	finger	foot
eye	throat	wrist	feet
mouth	arm	hip	ankle
		back	toe

Some sample sentences to be given in connection with the body:

1. Point to your nose.
2. I have blue eyes.
3. Wash your hands.
4. Brush your teeth.
5. I have brown hair.

```
┌──────────────────── Clothing ────────────────────┐
│                                                    │
│   shoes          suit            necktie           │
│   socks          dress           sweater           │
│   stocking       jacket          skirt             │
│   boots          shirt           blouse            │
│   rubbers        coat            gloves            │
│   pants          vest            hat               │
│                                                    │
└────────────────────────────────────────────────────┘
```

The clothing chart is connected with such verbs as "like," "will buy," "have," etc.

1. I have new brown shoes.
2. She has a new red dress.
3. I will buy boots.
4. I like your new hat.

Just as we put the letters together in our color speech system to form words, in the same manner we point to the words on the color charts to form sentences.

"I have new boots."

The teacher points to the pronoun chart for "I," the verb chart for "have," the adjective chart for "new," and the clothing chart for "boots."

We mentioned that language structure is very difficult for hearing-impaired children. In the beginning, when the child is trying to structure sentences, he should not have to struggle with the spelling of words. The color charts are there for him so that he can see the words that he wants to use, and they are easier for him to locate because he is looking for a particular color. The analogy system with which he is already familiar helps him to structure the sentences.

Using the Color Language Charts

We connect "like," "will eat," and "will buy" with food.

```
_____ Food _____
   meat          potatoes        pork
   eggs          milk            veal
   ham           sugar           beef
   butter        cake            turkey
   apples        pie             duck
   tomatoes      chicken         cheese
                 fish            bread
```

```
_____ Will Buy _____
   1. I will buy an apple.
   2. Larry will buy eggs.
   3. She will buy candy.
   4. My mother will cook ham.
   5. _____
```

Will Eat

1. I will eat apples.
2. Tami will eat bread **and** butter.
3. She will eat
4. _____
5. _____

Like

1. I like fish.
2. John likes apples.
3. My mother likes
4. _____
5. _____

"Can," "have," "like," "will buy," "will eat," "will play," "will go," "will work" and other such verbs must be given every day for the first month. The sentences formed from these verbs are fundamental for language development. Later on, we give this work only two or three times a week for the rest of the year.

The child has to write five or six sentences using the analogy system.

Adjectives

Adjectives can be connected with "verbs," "nouns," "pronouns," and with words such as those on the food or clothing charts. Therefore, we develop the adjective chart early with the following green words.

Adjectives		
good	low	strong
bad	fast	little
nice	slow	heavy
smart	big	light
stupid	small	dark
high	weak	new
		old

In every day communication with the children, you will employ new adjectives which can then be added to the chart. We use the adjectives with the analogy system in this way:

Big

1. The tree is big.
2. The horse is big.
3. The house is big.
4. _____
5. _____

Small

1. The bee is small.
2. _____
3. _____
4. _____
5. _____

The children now have five permanent charts. We make five columns and have the children write eight verbs, eight adjectives, etc.

Adjectives	Verbs	Clothing	Food	Body
1.				
2.				
3.				
4.				
5.				
6.				
7.				
8.				

These exercises are very helpful for memorization.

Negatives

We teach all negatives, such as "don't have," "don't like," "cannot," "will not" by means of the analogy system in the following way:

Cannot

1. I cannot fly.
2. I cannot cook.
3. _____
4. _____
5. _____

Don't Like

1. I don't like eggs.
2. I don't like fish.
3. _____
4. _____
5. _____

A Typical Day's Work

Most problem children have extremely short attention spans. They tire easily and have a tendency to become restless very quickly. A school day is a long working time for both teacher and children. The children's interest and attention must be held, and the time spent working with them must be worth-while and pleasant. It is necessary not to stay with one subject or activity for too long. Subject matter must be changed more frequently than it would if one were working with non-handicapped children.

Usually we begin our school day with speech, working with the phonetic sounds of the color alphabet. Following this some words are written on the blackboard, and the children must put these into color speech writing. (See color speech chart, p. 19) The children can write words using specific consonants or vowels (p. 19, 20) which the teacher chooses

Language teaching follows. The children write the News, work with the Analogy System (using various verbs, adjectives, etc.), and use the Crossbar System. When the language work is completed on the blackboard, the children re-enforce it by writing it in their notebooks. While the children are writing, we give auditory training to individual children (see p. 20).

The Crossbar System

The Crossbar System is important to language development. We have the children write the words in color on the left hand side of the cross. The sentences are written on the right. For the first few weeks the children should color the sentences.

For example:

	Verbs
1. come	1. I will go to gym.
2. go	2. I like chicken.
3. eat	3. I will play ball.
4. buy	4. My mother can cook.
5. have	5. The cow gives milk.
6. can	6.
7. like	7.
8. play	
9. work	
10. fly	
11. give	

	Adjectives
1. lazy	
2. good	
3. bad	1. Larry is strong.
4. fast	2. Today is cold.
5. slow	3. The horse is fast.
6. smart	4.
7. warm	5.
8. cold	6.
9. strong	7.
10. nice	

The Crossbar System can be given with clothing, money, pronouns, etc., since it structures the work and makes it easier to understand. When working with a new topic, the words can be given and explained by the teacher. The first two sentences can be worked out by the teacher and pupil together.

As previously mentioned, we color the sentences for the first few weeks. Later, we color the sentences only when the child seems to be confused with the structure.

	Animals
1. dog	
2. elephant	1. The horse is fast.
3. tiger	2. The elephant is big.
4. horse	3. I have a dog.
5. lion	4.
6. cow	5.
7. cat	

Question and Answer Forms

A very important part of language teaching is the question and answer form. Some questions have standard answers which the child can learn.

For example:

What is your name?
    My name is _____
How old are you?
    I am _____
How are you?
    I am _____
What is your address?

_____

_____

When will you go to gym?
    I will go to gym at 9:35.
What is the name of your school?

_____

Some questions must be thought out.
    Do you like bread?
    Will you go to the zoo?
    Will you go home?
    Can you jump?
    Can you drive?
    Will you play ball?
    Do you have a dog?

We give the question form which asks permission in the following way:

May I go_____ ?
1. May I go to art?
2. May I go to the bathroom?
3. May I go home?
4. _____
5. _____

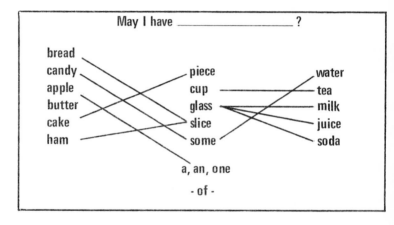

1. May I have a glass of milk?
2. May I have some candy?
3. May I have a cup of tea?
4. _____ ?
5. _____ ?

We have found the preceding chart very helpful for the children.

Weather

Each child should make pictures of the four seasons. We connect the seasons with the weather and make a weather chart.

Weather

windy	sunny	fine
foggy	rainy	lightning
hot	mild	stormy
warm	wet	hurricane
cold	**snowing**	thunder
cloudy	fair	shower
cool		

wind	. windy
cloud	. cloudy
sun	. sunny
rain	. rainy

The wind **is blowing.**
It **is windy.**

43

This is a thermometer.
It shows the temperature.
Today is 70° (degrees).
It is very pleasant.
I like it.
32° is the freezing point.
212° is the boiling point.
Freezing: The water becomes ice.
Boiling : Mother cooks an egg in the boiling water.

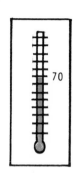

We give the weather with the Crossbar System.

Weather

1. cold
2. foggy
3. hot
4. rainy
5. warm
6. windy
7. pleasant
8. cloudy

1. March is windy.
2. Winter is cold.
3. Yesterday was rainy.
4. Spring is pleasant.
5. Today it is windy.

He will go home.
Will he go home?

Mary will go to gym.
Will Mary go to gym?

We use color with the question form to show the change sentence structure.

Teaching Time

The Color Clock)

Our children have had excellent results in telling time with our Color Clock and are able to transfer to a regular wall clock after a short period of time.

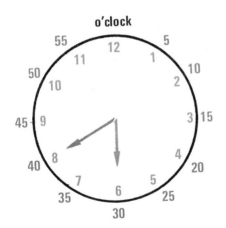

The short hand is red.
It points to the hour.
The long hand is blue.
It points to the minute.
Write the hours red, write the minutes blue this way:

3:30   6:40

We give the child sentences using the question form:
When?

When will you go to lunch?

When will you play ball?

When will you go to art?

The children may also question each other. We also give the question forms of What, Where, Who, etc. in this manner.

We teach the parts of the day in the following manner:

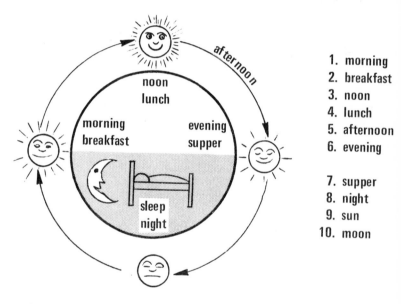

1. morning
2. breakfast
3. noon
4. lunch
5. afternoon
6. evening

7. supper
8. night
9. sun
10. moon

1. I eat breakfast in the morning.
2. I eat lunch at noon.
3. I eat supper in the evening.
4. I sleep at night.
5. _____
6. _____
7. _____

After exposing the children to the words on the drawing, we erase the words and have the children rewrite them.

Food

The following lessons can be given about food. (See food chart, p. 33.)

We have the children color each noun, verb, and adjective

meat	We have to eat to live.
vegetables	We eat meat, vegetables, and fruit. We also eat
fruit	butter and eggs.
butter	We drink milk.
eggs	We eat bread. Bread is made of wheat or rye.
bread	We get meat from the cow, sheep, and pig.
wheat	We eat beef from the cow.
rye	The meat of a young calf is called veal.
cow	The meat of a pig is called pork.
sheep	Potatoes, tomatoes, and beans are vegetables.
pig	There are many kinds of vegetables.
beef	The cow gives milk.
calf	Butter is made from milk.
veal	Cheese is made from milk.
pork	Apples, oranges, pears and bananas are fruits.
cheese	We eat chicken, duck, and turkey.
orange	My father likes fish.
pear	I like apples better than any other fruit.
banana	
chicken	
duck	
turkey	
fish	

	Food
1. bread	
2. meat	**1.** I like apples.
3. eat	**2.** I don't like fish.
4. fish	**3.** The apple is red.
5. lunch	**4.** I will eat bread **and** butter.
6. apple	**5.**
7. ham	
8. butter	
9. buy	

We drink - - - - - - - - - - -

Drink	
water	coffee
milk	tea
soda	milkshake
juice	7-Up
coke	lemonade

1. I am thirsty.
2. I want some milk.
3. Please bring me a cup of coffee.
4. May I have _____ .
5. Please give me _____ .
6. I don't like _____ .
7. Please give him _____ .

Teaching the Tenses

We make a chart using the past tense.

Present ▼	Past ◄	Present ▼	Past ◄	Present ▼	Past ◄
go	went	play	played	write	wrote
eat	ate	work	worked	give	gave
fly	flew	buy	bought	like	liked
see	saw	sleep	slept	cry	cried
fall	fell	wash	washed		
do	did	swim	swam		
get	got	drink	drank		
come	came	make	made		
have	had	take	took		

The children have the opportunity to use the past tense with many verbs through the news. However, this also needs special drill work. We have the children fill in the past and future tenses.

◄ Past	▼ Present	Future ➤
	go	
	eat	
	buy	
	play	
	have	
	like	

After the children have completed this drill, we put the following lesson on another blackboard. The children must write two sentences with:

will go

1. _____

2. _____

went ◄───

1. _____
2. _____

will eat ───►

1. _____
2. _____

ate ◄───

1. _____
2. _____

will play ───►

1. _____
2. _____

played ◄───

1. _____
2. _____

If the child masters the most important verbs then he will be able to apply them to the appropriate life situation.

We have found that it is helpful to use these symbols in the teaching of the tenses:

Future ───►

Present ↓

Past ◄───

Prepositions

Prepositions are a very important part of language structure. We always have the preposition chart before the children.

Prepositions:			
up	on	around	before
down	by	last	at
in	under	here	of
out	to	there	off
outside	for	same	with
inside	into	behind	over
near	away	where	
from	next	between	

Where is the pencil?

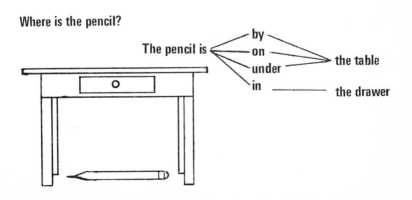

51

We draw an apple, a ball, a table, a chair, a house, and a tree.

1. The ball is on the chair.

3. The bird is above the house.

2. The ball is under the tree.

4. The apple is on the tree.

If the child is writing the news or relating a story and does not use the preposition, we ask him, "Where is the brown word?" If he does not know which preposition to use, we ask, "Which brown word will you use?"

We teach the prepositions with the Analogy and Crossbar Systems:

On
1. The apple is on the tree.
2. The pen is on the table.
3. The book is on the desk.
4. The cat is on the chair.
5. _____

Later, we have the children write different sentences using the prepositions.

On
1. The apple is on the table.
2. Put it on the chair.
3. We will go home on the bus.

We teach prepositions and prepositional phrases in the following manner:

The Tree

on the tree	1. _____
under the tree	2. _____
by the tree	3. _____
around the tree	4. _____
near the tree	5. _____
to the tree	6. _____

The Table

on the table	1. The bread is on the table.
under the table	2. The dog is under the table.
by the table	3. He is by the table.
around the table	4. The cat runs around the table.
above the table	5. The light is above the table.
from the table	6. _____

When teaching question forms, it is helpful to re-enforce the prepositions using What? and Where?

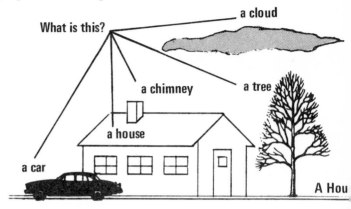

a cloud

What is this?

a chimney   a tree

a house

a car

A Hou

(Prepositions)

What
What is in front of the house?
What is above the house?
What is by the house?
What is on the house?

A Hil

Where
Where is the tree? (on)
Where is the apple? (on)
Where is the boy? (by)
Where is the bird? (above)
Where is the flower? (under)

Present Progressive

What do you see in the pictures?
What is he doing?
What is she doing?
What are they doing? (present progressive)

I see two girls.
They are playing ball.

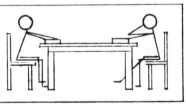

I see two men.
They are eating.

I see a bird.
It is flying.

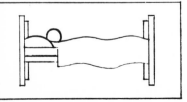

I see a boy.
He is sleeping.

I am eating.   **You are working.**   **He is swimming.**

What did Sue say?

Sue said, "I will go home."

Bob answered, "_____ _____."

What did Sue say? "_____."

What did Bob answer? "_____."

Pronoun Chart

Pronouns			To Be		
One			Present		Past
				One	
I	me	my			
you	you	your	I am		I was
he	him	his	you are		you were
she	her	her	he is		he was
it	it	its	she is		she was
			it is		it was
	Many			Many	
we	us	our	we are		we were
you	you	your	you are		you were
they	them	their	they are		they were

Teaching "is" and "are."
    The boy is in school.
    Is the boy in school?
    The boys are in the playground.
    Are the boys in the playground?

We have the child build similar sentences and questions with is and are.

Teaching "was" and "were."

It is very important to call the child's attention to the past tense of the verb "to be" whenever an actual situation arises. We write was and were on the blackboard in big letters. In subsequent lessons it may be taught as drillwork with the analogy system. I am, you are, he is, me, my, etc. may all be taught using the analogy system.

We teach "do" and "does" with questions and answers.

Q. Do you have any money?
A. I don't have any money.
Q. Do you like turkey?
A. Yes, I like turkey.
Q. Will you do me a favor?
A. Yes, I will do you a favor.
Q. Do you like baseball?
A. Yes, I do.
Q. Does he like baseball?
A. Yes, he does.
Q. Does she cook?
A. Yes, she does.

Some questions with "did."

Q. Did you eat supper?
A. Yes, I did.
Q. Did you buy a new hat?
A. No, I did not.

We build up language in a systematic way in order to make it easier for the centrally deaf child.

Commands and Phrases

We give the children commands and phrases which are used frequently:

Sit down, Get up, Come in, Go out, Open the window, door, etc., Close the door, Give me a pencil, Don't push me, Help me, Don't bother me, Stop it, What for?, How much?, How many?, What is it?

The child has to collect as many phrases as he can. We teach these through speech and auditory training. It also helps to have the children write these many times.

Reading Signs

We teach the child to read and understand signs which give information or which are important to their safety.

I see signs on the street
I see signs on the building.

What do these signs mean?

Exit	Bridge	Curve
Entrance	Danger	For Rent
Out of Order	No Smoking	Stop
No Vacancy	Subway	Go

Do you know any other signs?

We feel that the children must understand their responsibilities as citizens, and teaching them to read and understand signs gives them a sense of rules and regulations.

Re-enforcement of Verbs, Nouns, and Adjectives

The following sentences are useful for re-enforcing verbs, nouns, and adjectives. However, we find that it is best to allow the child to write complete sentences and not over emphasize the filling in of blanks, since the child will never acquire complete sentence structure in this manner.

Fill in the blanks with (verbs).

1. The horse can _____.
2. The bird can _____.
3. The children like to _____.
4. Father has to _____
5. I am going to _____.
6. I will _____ my lunch.
7. I _____ my mother.
8. I _____ (brown, blue) eyes.
9. I will _____ a bottle of soda.
10. Mother will _____ a new dress.

Fill in the blanks with (nouns).

1. I will buy a pair of _____ .
2. I will play with a _____ .
3. I will work with a _____ .
4. The table is made of _____ .
5. The hammer is made of _____ .
6. This is a _____ .
7. I will read a _____ .
8. I will write with a _____ .
9. I will eat a slice of _____ .
10. I will drink a cup of _____ .
11. May I have some _____ ?

Fill in the blanks with (adjectives).

1. The tree is _____ .
2. The boy is _____ .
3. I will get a _____ bird.
4. Mother will buy a _____ dress.
5. He is a _____ boy.

Teaching
the Calendar

We teach the days and the months of the year in connection with the Calendar. We have the child include the date each day in his "News." We also explain the New Year, Religious Holidays, and National Holidays as they arise during the school year.

We find that the following charts are very helpful to the children:

One Year has 12 months:	
1. January	7. July
2. February	8. August
3. March	9. September
4. April	10. October
5. May	11. November
6. June	12. December
	"Happy New Year"

One week has 7 days:

1. Sunday
2. Monday
3. Tuesday   Yesterday was _____
4. Wednesday   Today is _____
5. Thursday   Tomorrow will be _____
6. Friday
7. Saturday

1 month has 30 or 31 days
February has 28 or 29 days
1 year has 365 days
1 month has 4 weeks
1 week has 7 days

last week - next week - this month

We give the ordinal numbers with the days of the week and the months of the year:

January is the first month
February is the second month
March is the third month

Health

We usually have the children write something about health in their News. We also write short stories with the children when a situation involving health arises, using the Crossbar System. The short stories are very important as reading exercises.

	Health
1. sick	
2. doctor	1. Paul is sick.
3. cold	2. He has a cold.
4. cough	3. Paul went to the infirmary.
5. nurse	4. The nurse gave him some pills.
6. pills	5. I was sick too.
7. infirmary	6. I had a cough.
8. hospital	

```
                    Health Chart

    sick              healthy          ill
    doctor            a headache       not well
    nurse             an earache       felt sick
    drugstore         a toothache      I feel fine
    visit             a pain           wound
    a cold            medicine         operation
    a cough           pills            show me your
    a sore throat     hurt                tongue
```

Mastering the Language Forms

Write 10 different sentences.

1. The apple is on the tree.
2. I will buy a ball.
3. I like apples.
4. We will go to gym.
5. May I go to art?
6.
7.
8.
9.
10.

When the child is able to write ten different sentences, we know that he has mastered the various language forms.

Adjectives and Comparative Adjectives

Sue is a small girl.
Bob is a big boy.
____ is tall.
____ is short.

This is a small ball.
This is a big ball.
This is a bigger ball.
This is the biggest ball.

Which is the biggest ball?

strong	stronger	strongest
cold	colder	coldest
small	_____	_____
fast	_____	_____

It is strong. mouse, fly, elephant, dog, baby
It is big. Which is big? pencil, ring, dime, mountain

67

Which is the biggest ball?

Which is the smallest apple?

Which is round?   **Which is square?**

big   **bigger**   **biggest**

We give many comparisons in various ways. The child must see these many times.

Irregular Adjectives

We also give the irregular adjectives:

bad	worse	worst
good	better	best
much	more	most

We use dramatization for better understanding and encourage the child to give us comparisons of his own.

Reading Similar Sounding Numbers

We teach the children to hear, say, and read numbers to one hundred.

six	sixteen	sixty
seven	seventeen	seventy

Money

We teach the value of various articles with which the children are familiar, such as a pen, pencil, shoes, notebook, tie, shirt, etc.

We make a price list of vegetables, fruits, and other groceries. Visits to the supermarket, bakery, and butcher are helpful. An excellent opportunity for the children is to be taken to a restaurant where they can read the menu and order.

How much? (10) (10) (10) (10) (5) = 45¢

(25) (25) (10) = 60¢

(25) (10) (10) (5) = 50¢

How Many? How many eggs are in one dozen?
How many socks are in a pair?
How many socks are in 2 pairs?

Weights
and Measurements

We teach the measures of weight, length, and volume.
Measures of length . . . yard, meter, foot, inch, etc.
Measures of volume . . . gallon, quart, pint, etc.
Measures of time . . . year, month, week, day, hour, minute
etc.

We also teach "How many" with measurements.
1. How many feet in one yard?
2. How many ounces in a pound?
3. How many pints in a quart?
We use as many visual aids as possible.

We teach "How Much?" using money and measurements
1. If one yard costs 10¢, how much will you pay for three
   yards?
2. If one quart of milk costs 30¢, how much will you pay for
   two quarts?

"How much?" and "How many?" can be used in many dif
ferent ways.

Color
Teaching Devices

We use various teaching devices which have been formulated from our color system. The color teaching clock, the color play clock and the color map of the United States have been very successful in our teaching process. We also have a color watch which makes it easy for the children to tell time. In using the Color Map, the names of the States are written on matching colored flashcards. The teacher may also use white cards with the names of the States written in color. The white States written in black. One may also use the blackboard for this by writing the names of the States with colored chalk.

Color Map

Washington

Oregon

Idaho

Montana

North D

South

Nevada

Utah

Wyoming

Neb

Colorado

California

Arizona

New Mexico

O

Ohio

Texas

Nevada

72

e United States of America

Maine

Vermont
New Hampshire
Massachusetts

Wisconsin   Michigan

New York

Rhode Island

Connecticut

Pennsylvania

New Jersey

Ohio

West
Virginia

Delaware

Maryland

ta

wa

Illinois   Indiana

Virginia

Missouri

Kentucky

North Carolina

Tennessee

South
Carolina

Arkansas

Georgia

Mississippi

Alabama

Louisiana

Florida

Visual Arithmetic

Our method of teaching arithmetic in units of tens involves two different colors. The child can see what is happening when he adds or subtracts in colors. The four arithmetic fundamentals can be taught easily in this manner.

Use different shapes oo xx or colors.

+ Addition:

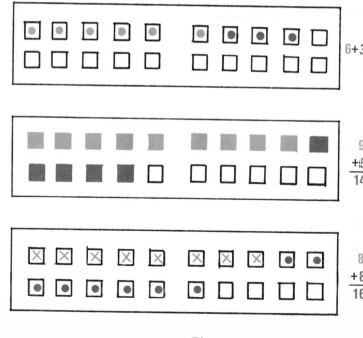

6+3=9

9
+5
14

8
+8
16

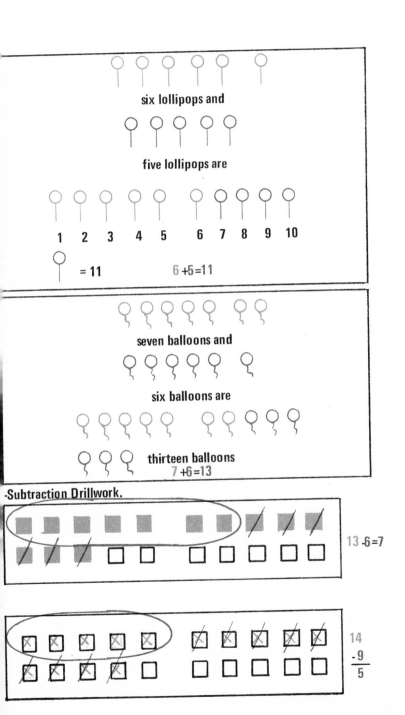

six lollipops and

five lollipops are

1 2 3 4 5   6 7 8 9 10

= 11   6 + 5 = 11

seven balloons and

six balloons are

thirteen balloons
7 + 6 = 13

-Subtraction Drillwork.

13 - 6 = 7

$$\begin{array}{r} 14 \\ -9 \\ \hline 5 \end{array}$$

75

You have 11 apples.

Take away 4 apples

How many apples are left?   7 apples

Multiplication

6x2=12

3x4=12

Division:

$$2\overline{\smash{)}10}^{\ 5}$$

$$3\overline{\smash{)}9}^{\ 3}$$

$$5\overline{\smash{)}10}^{\ 2}$$

Early Childhood (The First Steps)

To insure proper development, it is important to begin schooling early. During the preschool years the parents can play an important role by working with the child in order to develop him mentally, awaken his hearing and make him speech conscious. The parents can help the child with hearing development through proper auditory training because hearing development does not begin with speech sounds or words but with gross sounds which can awaken the child's auditory attention. We can use various noisemakers such as drums, whistles, horns, bells etc. to stimulate the child's hearing center. The child, as well as the teacher, must participate in the acoustical play. This helps to awaken the child's hearing through the Schwabach System which stimulates the hearing center through bone conduction. The vibration from the instruments which the child holds in his hand leads to the hearing center. Keep the child's hearing center stimulated first through gross sounds, then through speech. To utilize the child's different hearing sensitivity, use different frequencies with the instruments.

The child begins to understand his environment through expressive movements such as mimic, gesture and body movements. Through the expressive movements we begin to teach lipreading and simultaneously give auditory training to develop the child's hearing.

We begin by using the four word system (p.7) on flashcards containing the picture and word. Sometimes we must reduce the number of flashcards from four to two. If the child still has difficulty identifying the proper flashcard, then we must give the vowel sound of the word on the flashcard in picture form. For example: if we are using the word bee, then we draw the lip formation of $\bar{e}$ ⬠

The child should not feel pressured in any way and this work should be a form of play and enjoyment for him.

Hearing Tests and Hearing Aids

The centrally deaf child needs a specific way of testing his hearing. The pure-tone test is not valid for his type of deafness. Only after the child has some words in his speech-hearing center can he be tested for decibel hearing through speech discrimination. A centrally deaf child's response is inconsistent to hearing tests. One test will give remarkable hearing results, and another one will give a very poor response. These fluctuations are usually indicative of a centrally deaf child.

At the time of hearing awakening, when we begin to talk into the child's ear, we do not use a hearing aid on either ear. However, we do use a louder than normal voice. We mentioned that with stimulation the brain's compensating power will move to its physiological limit. At this time, a mild hearing aid may be used in order to give the child added stimulation for better hearing development. Most centrally deaf children will reject a strong aid. In our opinion, it is best to leave one ear without a mold at all times. The four-word system must always be used on the unaided ear.

Conclusion

We are faced with a time of great change in the education of the deaf. We cannot expect to educate the centrally deaf child with methods that apply to the inner ear deaf.

The aim of our book has been to help children with central speech and hearing imperception. The causes as to why so many children have this difficulty have not been thoroughly researched. The use of new drugs, birth control pills, tranquilizers, wartime traumas which damaged genes, drug addiction may all be possible contributing factors.

There are many theories pertaining to the workings of the human brain, and there will probably be many more. Our concern, as educators, must be to help the children who come to us. To do this, we need an understanding of the problem, methods that work, patience, and a lot of love. The development of effective methods are desperately needed. We have given you a theory and our method which is based on this theory using our color system. It has had excellent results for many years with problem children.

Schools for the deaf must open their doors for the centrally deaf children. Teachers trained with a proper approach and method will be able to help them. They must be familiar with their emotional and learning problems, and be aware of the fact that these children are not multiple handicapped. In most cases, their so-called multiple handicaps are but manifestations of their central hearing problem. Today, the hearing schools have their share of children with emotional and learning difficulties which are caused by various forms of central imperception, including speech and hearing. If a proper approach and method are used and the child begins to develop mentally, these so-called multiple problems will disappear.

Schools need administrators who know the problems and how to approach them. Teachers are in desperate need of help in order to meet these problems which have been multiplying for the past decade but which have not received the necessary attention. It is the responsibility of the administration of the school to help alleviate the situation.

A special diagnostic class is needed for new admissions to the school. This class should have a teacher who is capable of placing the children according to their problem.

A curriculum must be worked out for the first two years of the elementary level. It is necessary that the children have a workbook, a first reading book, and tapes which have auditory training lessons with the four-word system. The tapes should be on such practical everyday topics as health, weather, food, clothing, etc. These tapes can be helpful during the summer months, since the centrally impaired child has a tendency to regress if he has no contact with educational training.

Discipline is a very important aspect of our work. The child must have consistency, and clear lines must be drawn between acceptable and unacceptable behavior. It is very important for the children to be able to work together as a group. To isolate a child in a cubby or to work with him individually because his concentration or behavior is such as not to allow him to work with his classmates only serves to re-enforce the problem. He must be taught how to get along with his peers. If one child is able to progress at a faster pace, then he can be given more advanced work. An important aspect of successful living is to be able to work with and get along with others. If we wish to integrate our children into society as acceptable adults, then the learning of acceptable group behavior is necessary at an early age.

We offer you a method that has worked for us consistently and for a long time. It has proven itself by its results and stands ready to help the many teachers who care about their children but who are at a loss to teach effectively. Other methods will surely be developed. However, this method offers the groundwork for your variation and enhancement based on a sound and successful program.

Biographical Sketches

Ernest Tinsmith received his elementary school teacher's diploma in 1923 from the Lutheran College for Elementary School Teachers in Hungary. He attended the Royal Hungarian College for the Education of Professors of the Healing-Pedagogy and received his professor's diploma in 1927. In Hungary, he was superintendent of the Komarom State School for the Deaf, which he reorganized. He then organized and became superintendent of the Loshonc State School. In 1948, he organized a State School in Salzburg, Austria, where he was Educational Department Head and teacher trainer. He started to work with cortical speech and hearing problems beginning in 1924, after studying and observing the work of Dr. Gustav Barczi. He has continued his work uninterruptedly since then. Professor Tinsmith came to the United States in 1950. He attended Columbia University and was a student-teacher at the Lexington School for the Deaf in 1952-53. He became a speech therapist at the New York Eye and Ear Infirmary for the express purpose of proving brain deafness to the medical profession. Professor Tinsmith was teaching problem children at The New York School for the Deaf for the past fifteen years with excellent results. For his successful teaching results he received a certificate of merit for distinguished achievement from The Conference of Executives of American Schools for the Deaf and The Convention of American Instructors of the Deaf. He has also been made an Honorary Life Member of The N.Y.S.A.E.D. His contributions to hearing impaired children have also been met with gratitude and appreciation from The Alexander Graham Bell Association for the Deaf. Ernest Tinsmith and Katherine J. Martens have lectured about the problems confronting today's educators of the deaf at: The New York State Association of Educators of the Deaf Convention at Rome, N.Y. 1971 on "Ungraded Classes The Problem Deaf Child" and at The New York State Association of the Deaf Convention at Grossinger's, N.Y. 1972. Program Theme: "Educating Today's Atypical Deaf Child" Lecture! "The Centrally Deaf Child—A New Approach and The Color System."

Dr. Gustav Barczi, noted Hungarian otolaringologist and teacher of the deaf, began his experiments with cortical speech and hearing problems in 1922. He called his system "Surdomutitas Corticalis" (Deaf Muteness in the Cortex). He reported the results of his experimentations for the first time at the International Congress of Logopedia in Budapest, Hungary, in 1934. His first book on Surdomutitas Corticalis was published in 1935. Many publications and translations followed. In 1951, the landmark medical text, *The Acta Oto Laringologica Supplementum 96,* a book about auditory training systems by Dr. Eric Wedenberg, cited Dr. Barczi's contribution as unique and exceptional.

Katherine J. Martens received her B.A. Degree from Adelphi University. Prior to entering the Education of the Deaf, she was a teacher of hearing children in New York City. As the parent of a deaf child, she has a very personal interest in the education of the deaf. After training with Professor Tinsmith, she can understand clearly what the problems are but more importantly how to approach them. It is her hope that this book will ease the confusion and give encouragement to parents, teachers and children.